LAUREN BACALL SHARES A LIMOUSINE

LAUREN BACALL SHARES A LIMOUSINE

Poems by Susan J. Erickson

BRICK ROAD
POETRY PRESS

Cover art: "Rapunzel" © Catrin Welz-Stein

Author photo: Susan J. Erickson portrait by Diane Padys
©dianepadysphotography.com

Thank you to artist Nancy Canyon who created the sketch for the interior
pages of the book. © 2013

Library of Congress Control Number: 2016954507
ISBN-13: 978-0-9898724-9-2

Published by Brick Road Poetry Press
513 Broadway
Columbus, GA 31902-0751
www.brickroadpoetrypress.com

Brick Road logo by Dwight New

*This book is dedicated to the women within it
and to all women who live above nerve*

If your Nerve, deny you—
Go above your Nerve—

—Emily Dickinson

Acknowledgments

Many thanks to the editors of the following publications where these poems first appeared, sometimes in earlier versions or with different titles:

2River View: "Casa Azul" and "Frida Kahlo Prepares an Altar for *Día de los Inocentes*, Day of the Innocents"

Bellingham Herald: "Faye Wray Tweets atop the Empire State Building"

Blast Furnace: "Miss O'Keeffe Makes Pea Soup"

Bloodstone Review: "What Marilyn Monroe Tells Her Dressmaker While Fitting Her 'Mr. President' Gown."

Cactus Heart Literary Magazine: "Sleeping with Trotsky" and "Georgia O'Keeffe Hitches a Ride to Abiquiu"

Crab Creek Review: "A Dozen or So Reasons Zelda Offers for Marrying Scott Fitzgerald Interspersed with Lines by Edna St. Vincent Millay"

Empowerment 4 Women: "Lady Godiva Reminisces"

Fiolet & Wing: An Anthology of Domestic Fabulist Poetry: Forthcoming: "Venus de Milo Gets Ready for the Halloween Party"

Forgotten Women: An Anthology by Grayson Books. Forthcoming: "Monique Braille's Confession" and "Nurses of Bataan, Prisoners of War, The Third Year"

Hamilton Stone Review: "Advice from Miss Nancy" and "Before Her Round-the-World Flight Amelia Visits with a Psychic"

jabberwock review: "Zelda Fitzgerald is Banned from Baby Scottie's Baptism, St. Paul, Minnesota, 1921"

James Franco Review: "Marilyn Monroe Imagines Her Life as Menu Items at Schrafft's" and "Marilyn Monroe Sits for Andy Warhol in the Afterlife"

Labyrinth: "Pantoum for Mata Hara"

Literal Latte: "Frida and Frankenstein"

Love Over 60: an anthology of women's poems: "Madame Matisse Writes from Troyes Prison"

Marathon Literary Review: "Mamah Borthwick Cheney Goes Abroad with Frank Lloyd Wright"

Naugatuck River Review: "Frida's Clothesline"

Nonbinary Review: "Mr. Wizard,"

Poem Your Heart Out, Volume 2: From the Poetic Asides Poem-a-Day Challenge: "After Dorothy Gale's Mid-Life Crisis"

Raven Chronicles: "Elizabeth Barrett Takes Up Tweeting"

San Pedro River Review: "Janis Joplin Buys Her First Record Albums"

Sin Fronteras: "Georgia O'Keeffe Paints Cebolla Church, 1945"

Smoky Blue Literary and Arts Magazine: "Field Notes of Lucy Bakewell Observing the Eastern Phoebe with John James Audubon, 1804;" "Lucy Audubon Tends Her Husband after His Second Stroke, 1847" and "Zelda Fitzgerald Writes *Save Me the Waltz* in Phipps Clinic, 1932"

Sweet Tree Review: "Rapunzel Brings Her Women's Study Class to the Tower"

The Fourth River: "Miss O'Keeffe at the Black Place," "Miss O'Keeffe at the White Place" and "Georgia O'Keeffe Divides the Iris"

The Lyric: "Ballad of Frida and Diego" and "Emily Dickinson Observes Lent"

The Museum of Americana: "Self-Portrait as Janis Joplin's Porsche," "Lucy Audubon Wearies of Poverty and Her Husband's Rambling Ways, 1821," "In New Orleans, the Audubons Sit for Silhouette Cuttings, 1825" and "Confession of Sarah Rosetta Wakeman, Also Known as Private Lyons Wakeman, 153rd Regiment, New York State Volunteers, Union Army"

The Tishman Review: "Lauren Bacall Shares a Limousine to the Afterlife with Robin Williams"

Till the Tide: An Anthology of Mermaid Poetry: "The Little Mermaid at the Aquatic Arts Academy (AAA)" and "Advisory Letter: Little Mermaid to Errant Lover"

"Casa Azul" was reprinted in *Not Somewhere Else But* Here: *A Contemporary Anthology of Women and Place*:

"Miss O'Keeffe Makes Pea Soup" was reprinted in *Pontoon 2015* and in *Noisy Water: Poetry from Whatcom County, Washington*

"Elizabeth Barrett Takes Up Tweeting" was nominated for a 2015 Pushcart Prize by the editors of *Raven Chronicles*

Contents

Frida Kahlo

Lucy Audubon

Zelda Fitzgerald

Georgia O'Keeffe

Janis Joplin

Marilyn Monroe

Frida Kahlo

Casa Azul

From the spectrum of ghosts, I painted
this house blue to guide my father
and mother to my door. They sit
with Diego and me in the yellow kitchen.
Papa's hands tremble
as he lights my cigarette.
Mama trails the scent
of incense from evening mass.

Papasito hides
behind his camera.
He records the portraits of our shadow
selves—the ones we want
the mirror to reflect. Papa reminds me,
Do not smile. You seduce the camera.

At Mama's feet, the dogs
lick crumbs of *pan dulce*
from her fingers. She fusses
about the kitchen. From the strongbox
of her chest she pulls
a white handkerchief and bandages
my painting to soak up its blood.
Her rosary beads click, bones breaking.

She is tired of my gashes and scars.

When she returns to the spirit world,

I reopen the wounds, the palette

from which I paint myself.

This house of cobalt

is the womb where I will die. For years

Death and I have played

at the game of *exquisite corpse*.

Before my first Communion, Death drew

my withered leg. I counter,

sketching my heart. See

how it palpitates in my bare hands?

Frida Kahlo Prepares an Altar
for *Día de los Inocentes*

The sugar skulls that honor my babies
are tiny skeletons of doves fallen

from the thorn trees onto the patio
of the Blue House. No sugar letters

spell out names on the skulls.
My broken body took each baby

from me before I knew if it were he
or she. The nest of my pelvis, tossed

and pierced, is flimsy as sticks thrown together
by doves to cradle their young. For my *angelitos*

I bring a toy truck, tin whistles, cardboard puppets,
a baby's gold necklace. I raid the garden

of marigolds, string them into garlands
to drape over the altar, bright as lights

around a carnival ride. Their fragrance, bold
as mariachi trumpets—who can sleep?

Tonight sit with me. Drink tequila.

Sing for the *Inocentes*, yours and mine.

When it's time for them to slip back

to the spirit world, we will kiss them on the lips

of their souls, where Death dares not touch.

We will pour a shot for Death. And laugh.

Frida's Clothesline

Diego's underpants, pegged on the line,
flap like pink surrender flags. My Diego
is a *gordito*. The mercantile does not stock his size
in underwear. I have them made to his measurements,
which are secret, of course.

Diego's appetites are as big as his belly—
not even pink undershorts deter his conquests.
For years I've tried to goad Diego into fidelity.
But I am the surrendering party. I should grab
a pair of his underwear from the line and wave them
like a bullfighter's faded muleta.

Instead I sit in his lap, feed him
his favorite squash cake in small cubes
from my fingers. Like a baby.
Diego *is* my baby. He pat, pat, pats,
his belly as if he were carrying our child.
He leaves only crumbs for the monkeys.
What a glutton!

Diego did not promise me
faithfulness, but loyalty. Now with my own hands,
in the colors of the Mexican flag, I embroider

his pink percale with that vow. The prick
of the needle? I shrug it off.

While I stitch, I sing that song Diego likes so much,
"*La Bruja.*" I do not hum its melody. I shout its words.
Listen, Diego, listen:
"Oh tell me, oh tell me, oh tell me please!
How many children have you sucked dry of life?"

The scissors sigh.   I stitch L.   Then O,
in stitches that can never be pulled out.

Frida and Frankenstein

Frankenstein, poor fellow, is a piñata
molded and pasted from bits and pieces:
brown leather boot, stick of dynamite,
flayed skin, piano key teeth, brain
snatched from formaldehyde,
and a tarnished tinsel heart.

His fate? To be knocked and smashed
for the fun of destruction. I've seen this movie
more than once. But today, I show
Frankenstein my damaged paw. He steps
from the screen, lumbers down the dark
theatre aisle, kneels before my seat and asks

I come away with him, be his companion.
We slip outside the theatre, along
an alleyway to a small hotel, take a room
overlooking the street women at work.
I tell the story of how I became a monster
in one afternoon. I show him patches

and stitches, the zipper of saw marks
on my spine. Oh, damn, he is sobbing. Even he
understands it's not going to work.

I dry his tears and send him back
to his black and white life.

Sleeping With Trotsky

El Viejo. I called him *El Viejo*—old man—
because he was. Old. And because his goatee
and hair were white and wispy
like the old man cactus in the garden
at the Blue House.

And I called him *Piochitas*—
little goatee—because I tugged
at his beard when he shot
words at me as if I were a revolutionary
against the execution wall.

With the same rapid-fire delivery,
Trotsky, ex-commander of the Red Army,
made love like an item on his to-do list.
He should have enrolled in the History
of Frida and Diego's Love Life.

I could recite dates, names, battles, truces
of that ongoing war. Sleeping with Trotsky
was my offensive move for Diego's audacity
in bedding my sister. Should I have warned
an old man that Diego threatened to shoot traitors?

I sent *El Viejo* off for further study of cacti,

to enlarge his collection of exotic species.

Let him admire their flowers, wrestle

with their spines, stay up late to see

the night-bloomers, watch them wilt.

The Ballad of Frida and Diego

"Diego, this portrait is for you
our fifteen years entwined.
Its single head, half you, half me—
the features misaligned,
our psyches misaligned.

Our brows like birds' disjointed wings
fly over eyes askew
our lips contort in fractured kiss
the me that's not quite you,
the us that's split in two.

A common necklace binds us tight
with branch that's lost its leaves
its roots enmesh both shell and conch
where sun and moon still cleave,
both you and I now cleave.

In black fedora the murderer
with dagger in his grip,
surveys his love awash in blood:
I took A Few Small Nips,
only a few small nips.

Your razor charm and green sword eyes
captured my sister's bed.
Betrayal takes its own small nips
the wounds concealed inside,
still bleed and scar inside.

I paint Two Fridas I've become:
one in *Tehuna* dress
your portrait tethered to my heart
accelerates my pulse.
Diego is my pulse.

The other dressed in bridal white
with sectioned heart exposed
my blood cascades from severed vein
my beings juxtaposed,
two beings juxtaposed."

This ballad ends as many do
when truth and myth collide
as Frida dies and yields her flesh
Diego at her side,
obsession gratified.

Your sacred ashes I consume
my dear niña Frida.
My being finally melds with yours,

cries, Viva la Vida!
cries, Viva la Frida!

Madame Matisse Writes from Troyes Prison

Dear HM,

How delighted I should be to have a brilliant green nose
dabbed with yellow, as you once painted me. I am ravenous
for color, for light in this gray place. Sometimes if I close
my eyes tightly, I can see orange, see the oranges
piled in that basket you painted in Tangiers.
How did Picasso end up with *Corbeille d'oranges*?
Tell him I need orange more than he.

Of Marguerite, I know only she was arrested near Brest
and jailed in Rennes. Henri, remember, she's as strong
as your Nice sun, as steady as the metronome
which sat on our piano. She is a seashell. When she
        returns,
hold her to your ear. You will hear what to do.

Are you dismayed you knew nothing about our work
with the Resistance? We wanted to spare you.
It would have troubled your spirit, you who dream
of art as a good armchair. But I confess, we wanted
to be remembered as more than models in your paintings.

The Nazi fire has spread across our country,
but it is only a matter of time

until it will be extinguished.

You know, Henri, I am in my element
when the house burns down.

Of course, there is also *our* war to speak of.
Perhaps we can never again be allies, but could we not
declare an armistice?

Paint, Henri, paint. I am counting on you
to keep the color burning.
Amélie

Confession of Sarah Rosetta Wakeman, Also Known as Private Lyons Wakeman, 153rd Regiment, New York State Volunteers, Union Army

Truth of it, I was big as those Boys

barely into long pants.

My hair was short cut.

The recruitment man didn't bat an eye

when I stretched my nineteen years

to twenty-one; he was mighty glad

to have Lyons Wakeman sign up.

The only ones ever caught on

were the women like me—bound

and determined to reap the rewards of soldiering.

That *100 and 52 $ in money* I got for enlisting

was more than I ever did make at one time.

Leaving home, I figured to be a lot more help

than staying on the farm Pining for some man

to marry me. In this regiment,

I was *independent as a hog on ice.*

I traveled to the united states capitol

and been inside of it. You better believe

it is a pretty place.

I have got So that I Can drill just as well
as any man there is in my regiment.
For my part… I think a Skirmish drill
is the prettiest drill that ever was drill.

We was on water for nine days
on the Steam Ship Mississippi
coming to this state of Louisiana.
Then we marched near seven hundred miles
through Rebel country. Rations hard
to come by, we drunk swamp water.

We was in that Battle of Pleasant Hill
which I can report was not pleasant.

Still, I liked *to be a soldier very well.* I only wish
I'd been shot dead on the field of battle
rather than suffer this accursed dysentery.
I am feared it will be the death of me.

> Respectfully,
> Rosetta Wakeman
> In the month of June, 1864

Nurses of Bataan, Prisoners of War, the Third Year

Slowly starving,

our legs thinned to bamboo stalks

or swelled like palm tree trunks.

We and those we nursed

suffered anemia, beriberi, scurvy,

pellagra—the diseases of deprivation.

The lucky ones stopped menstruating,

saving us from the public task

of washing and drying homemade

fabric pads embroidered with our initials.

We ate okra and greens fried

in cold cream from Red Cross kits,

traded recipes rich in fat and calories,

planned fantasy menus.

Within the prison walls, sparrows,

pigeons, and cats disappeared. Thanksgiving dinner

was a ladleful of rice, a cup of vegetable stew

and a spoonful of *camote* tops.

Work was our meat of survival,

sunsets and moonlight our art.

Hope was a rag doll named Any-Day-Now,

in a uniform of khaki scraps,

liberated, too, when the gates crashed down.

Photographs from Number Three
Erla Work Camp

Germany, April 1945

It was necessary

    to draw the veil

        tightly

over my mind,

to give up being

    Margaret Bourke-White,

        become

nameless

    like the dead.

It was necessary

    to put the camera

        between

myself and what was revealed:

    blackened bodies

        some with an arm

                stretched beneath

    coiled barbed wire

charred rib cages

    graniteware feeding bowls

a scattering

    of

        spoons

Pantoum for Mata Hari

She choreographed life like an exotic dance,
swinging beads and swirling veils to fool the eye.
Dancing and dying should be performed with style,
Mata Hari boasted, then proved it true.

With swinging beads and swirling veils that fool the eye,
a woman can seduce high society—
Mata Hari boasted and proved it true.
The French adored her unclothed panache.

A woman like Mata seduced high society
and men with egos and money in their pockets.
How the French adored her naked panache
until they needed a scapegoat for a war gone wrong.

Men with egos and power in their pockets
denounced and jailed her as a German spy.
Needing a scapegoat for a war gone wrong,
they convicted Mata Hari: the Eye of the Day.

Denounced and convicted as a German spy,
before a firing squad of twelve Zouaves,
Mata Hari stood at the eye of the day.
Refusing to be bound, she stared and waved.

Before a firing squad of twelve Zouaves,

she choreographed life like an exotic dance.

Refusing to be bound, she stared and waved.

Shouldn't dying and dancing be performed with style?

Lady Godiva Reminisces

He said wars were expensive

He said his spies reported that nearby city-states were arming
    themselves

Diabolic weapons were invented every day he warned

He said as a major power in the world, sacrifices were necessary

He said he valued his family and country beyond measure

He said, yes, there would be new taxes

Yes, the people consider it an honor to pay taxes

He said people complain no matter what a Leader does

He said his advisors were brilliant, no one had ever taxed horses
    before

God, he said, was his Commander-in-Chief, or was it vice versa

He said Look, woman, ride down the street midday in the
    altogether

and then I'll lower taxes

I remember mother saying this was going too far

She said obedience was a virtue I should pray for

I remember the maid let down my hair and brushed it six hundred
    strokes

I remember my horse's coat gleamed, too

I remember my robe slipping to the ground

Pink valerian bloomed along the stone walls

I remember the cottages shuttered as if a storm was coming

I remember a Peacock butterfly resting on my foot

The next day, citing positive political polls, he issued a tax rebate

I remember hearing clapping, or maybe it was laundry snapping in
the wind

Lucy Audubon

Field Notes of Lucy Bakewell Observing the Eastern Phoebe

with John James Audubon, 1804

Early April. The sugar maple buds are fat.
Soft sheen of pussy willows
near Perkiomen Creek. Reverent as pilgrims
we come to the cave. At its arched entrance
the phoebes, peewees he calls them,
have anchored a nest the size
of Mr. Audubon's cupped hand.

The birds are as trusting as friends. I expect
them to light on his fingers or perch
on a shoulder. Like them, I am charmed
by this man I call LaForest and imagine
settling into the hollow of his shoulder.

Fee-bee, fee-bee, fee-b-be-bee the male courts
the silent female. Father, bless him,
favors such quietude on my part. But
docility is not my nature. I resort
to melodic responses on my pianoforte.

Before the young fledge, I nest each one
in my hand. LaForest ties a silvered thread
around the leg. Fortunate birds

carry Audubon's mark. I admit,

I desire such a band on my life.

Lucy Audubon Mourns the Daughter Named after Her and Her Mother before Her

Water on the brain

    dropsy of the head

        hydrocephalus.

Such weighty labels

    for the baby

        we named Lucy.

The black vulture of death

    hovered

        for two years—

landing, it feeds at our hearts.

Lucy Audubon Wearies of Coping with Poverty and Her Husband's Rambling Ways, 1821

Hopes are shy birds flying at a great distance.
Your remark, dear husband, is also true

of money which flies Away From
not toward this family. Our two young sons

(shall they be clothed in feathers?)

and I fend for ourselves while you—
great-footed hawk, black-bellied darter,

magnolia warbler—migrate in pursuit
of Ornithological obsessions. From New Orleans

you send me Queen's Ware dishes. Oh, John,
I am anything but queenly:

no table of my own to set, family silver
gone to bankruptcy, four teeth pulled.

In New Orleans, the Audubons Sit for Silhouette Cuttings, 1825

Swift and sure as a swallow,
Mr. Edwards' scissors dart

snip, snip
in and out

along the black paper. *Voila!*
The countenance of my husband
emerges—

at his neck, soft curls
combed by my fingers
clipped with my scissors
forehead of a dreamer
Gallic nose from his papa
chin of a determined general.

We are agreed—John must go.
Soon he will sail to England.
Our nation cannot engrave his life-sized
vision: *The Birds of America.*

My turn. I sit still.
The scissors know only

the shape of what is,

not what will be.

Lucy Audubon Tends Her Husband
after His Second Stroke, 1847

John's *great maxim* in drawing birds—

place them on a center of gravity.

But his own locus is off kilter.

Birds have flown from his head.

Now he obsesses about eating—

rings the dinner bell: clang, clang!

Again a half hour later. Teeth gone,

I feed him coddled eggs

and bread soaked in warm milk.

Clang, clang!

At night he begs for his little French song.

Georgianna, our sweet-voiced daughter-in-law,

sings for him:

Au clair de la lune

On n'y voit qu'un peu. . .

Under the moonlight

Little can be seen.

Lucy Audubon in the Boarding House, 1865

Pull a wire and the kingfisher's wing lifted.

Another wire elevated its tail

to full alert or turned its head

so the bird looked poised to dive

for a brown trout fry. John James'

mounting invention let him position

a just-killed bird as if still alive.

Wires. String. Artifice. Nothing

bound money to our pockets.

No device returns John and my boys to life.

I am relegated to this boarding house

where the tea is as weak as my future,

the days so quiet I hear the wingbeats

of my thoughts:

I have under errour and ignorance

sacrificed John's original paintings

for his Birds of America

       (for a pittance)

and their copper engraving plates

       (again, a pittance).

Before Her Round-the-World Flight
Amelia Visits With a Psychic

I'm licensed in the aerodynamics

of death, have fought its drag and thrust

when the double face of up and down

clouded the horizon. Now do I taunt death?

> *The sharp tang of whiskey*
> *slurs the vision of the man mapping*
> *your way around the world's waist.*

People imagine fear as a parachute

to keep one safe. They are wrong.

When I was seven I took my new sled

to the top of the hill, belly-slammed down,

slid under a horse and wagon, then waved

to my sister, frozen at the crest of the hill.

> *Luck is a mirage on a hot runway,*
> *a ripple-splash of water*
> *which never quenches thirst.*

If this flight is my time to pop off, luck aside,

I could crash—wings crumple—

in some pasture fragrant with spearmint
and fuel oil where a black-and-white cow
will wash my abandoned calf face
preparing me for what comes next.

> *You've mothered a mother, Amelia.*
> *Would you accept the tenderness*
> *of a rough tongue?*

Perhaps I'll descend onto a field
where ghosts greet me with a handshake,
no medals hung around my neck,
I'll wear only a string of pearls.

> *Again and again you've launched*
> *into headwinds. You know, don't you,*
> *your name means work and effort?*

But my plotted course may swerve
like the Lost Star of the Pleiades,
and my Electra may disappear
into a vastness beyond the earth's grip.

> *For now, hold my hand.*

Edna St. Vincent Millay Gives Herself Advice

Never speak in that sick voice
monotonous as a rocking chair.
Keys corrode atop the bureau.
You are not in thrall to Bluebeard,

go outside every day. Give up
biting your nails. Never let anyone
see you slip the hypodermic
into your thirsty vein.

Your pant of relief and skill
with the needle—its aim sure
as William Tell—make it obvious
the syringe is a lover

more demanding
than a sonnet's turn.

Monique Braille's Confession

As gentle as a beguilement of butterflies,
my son's fingertips read the alphabet
of my face. I erase the punctuation
of worry from my brow. The scent
of tears disturbs Louis, so I divert
mine to water the radishes.

My habit is to kiss first
Louis' right eye—the one he punctured
playing with Simon-Rene's awl.
Then I kiss the left, blinded
by disease, as if I were Saint Lucy
and could miraculously bestow sight.

Between the pages of my Bible,
I keep the holy card from Father Palluy
where Saint Lucy displays
a gold platter with two eyeballs
balanced like plump grapes
from our vineyard. Should Lucy appear
I would demand she earn her holy keep.

(I make the Sign of the Cross

for I do not intend sacrilege.

Do I?)

Whatever the weather, I wear

the tight-button collar of guilt.

At every chance, I read to Louis,

but always there is butter to churn,

chickens that need heads cut off.

Louis is my favorite child. Today

he leaves for the Royal Institute in Paris

where it is said they open the eyes

of the blind, lead them through

the doors of darkness.

I am not a wheel on the carriage

that takes Louis away, nor the ridged

track left in the mud. I am the patched

elbow of the republic of motherhood.

Mamah Borthwick Cheney Goes Abroad with Frank Lloyd Wright

I do not want my children

to see through the dirty windows

of my words. *I'm going on a vacation*

I tell them.

I vacate the cottage

of motherhood. Steal off

while the children sleep,

their bodies rising and falling

with the sweet faith of gravity.

Martha sucks her thumb. Beside her,

John lies toy soldier straight.

If the children clung,

one to each of my legs, sobbing,

would I still

pry loose their sweaty fingers and walk away

into Frank's arms?

I dismantle the house

of marriage where Edwin and I posed

at opposite ends of a table.

He will serve me forgiveness

like a broiled chop on a gilt-edged platter.

Frank flees

six children, his wife of two decades.

We sail for Europe with no blueprint

for the architecture of our lives.

Our first night together all I can do

is hold Frank's hand. Then we are swallowed

by the rhythms of the sea.

       Through the porthole,

the shore gone;

against the ship,

the steady shove of waves.

Kitty Wright Rehearses for an Interview with the Chicago Tribune Reporter after Frank Lloyd Wright Deserts His Family to Go Abroad

When the Trib reporter asks: *Is it true,*
Mrs. Wright, that Mrs. Cheney is a family friend?

I'll reply: That woman is a vampire
who latched onto Frank.
She seduced him.

Mr. Reporter's pencil lead will break.
He'll paw in his breast pocket
for a sharpened replacement. By that time,
      (admiring my titan hair)
he'll be a bit in love with me
for guaranteeing him a byline
on tomorrow's front page.

He'll hear newsboys shout
from every street corner:
Read all about it. Vampire. Vampire.
Mrs. Wright calls Mrs. Cheney a Vampire.

I'll go on: Frank is my Romeo.
I am Juliet. I await his return.
Our six children wait with me.

I've learned a few tricks

from Frank's performances—

swirling cape, cane brandished

like a scepter of lightning. I'll steer

his yellow-devil roadster into a cul-de-sac.

I won't be an outmoded design

in the Frank Lloyd Wright portfolio.

Mrs. Cheney is a sketch on an envelope.

I'm the wife. Ink cannot be erased.

Vita Sackville-West, Diary Entry, 1955

That bit about the moon inspiring the White Garden at
Sissinghurst? Not total poppycock. Who doesn't sail off in an
unmoored skiff in the trawl of a full moon? I could hardly admit to
the readers of my gardening column that I wish to memorialize the
pale skin of a lover's thighs with the *Regale* lilies. Good gardeners
would then ask for genus and species: *Woolfe virginiaus*, etc., etc. I
dare not suggest the ivory *eremurus* replicates the spine of every
woman I have loved. Nor could I reveal how the petals of the tree
peony remind me of a curve of creamy breast. Both Harold and I
have dirt under our fingernails. The tangled roots of our marriage
are mulched in contradiction. Yet we created what Harold calls a
true portrait of a marriage where thorned roses ramble and cast
perfume on the indifferent air.

Maman

30 foot steel and marble spider sculpted in 1999
by Louise Bourgeois as an ode to her mother

The first action any female takes with her eggs is to swathe
them in silk.

Mother kept me swathed in silk until Father went off
to war. We visited him in hospital: saw limbs detached
from owners, looked away from rag doll faces with scarred
cheeks, noses out of place, eyes unbuttoned, torn faces that
        would
never be mended. Father came home, threads tangled,
handsome as ever on the outside.

Spiders are set apart from all other animals by their universal
ability to spin silk.

My mother repaired tapestries. I learned to draw on canvas
restoring missing fragments for the weavers. Feet. Legs.
I became an expert on drawing feet and legs. I gave Maman
legs of steel to elevate her above the earth.

The web acts as the communication line during courtship.
The male begins by delivering a series of gentle tweaks
to the web in such a manner that the female recognizes
the coded signals.

My mother ignored coded signals. Sadie appeared
after the war to teach my brother and me. Sadie's breasts
were ripe melons she shared with my father. She patted us,
well-behaved dogs, as if she were our mistress too.

Although spiders have multiple eyes, most species have poor
vision.

Maman was blind to this intruder. She was mute
and blind when father, at table, cut the skin of an orange
with a razor in the outline of my figure. He would lay
back the fruit segments leaving the pith like a penis.
Then he would announce, "Well, this is not my daughter
because she doesn't have very much there."

Spiders are the most successful terrestrial predators.

Darkness is our natural habitat, isn't it, Mother?
Let others sleep beneath woolen blankets
of trust. I am hungry for the succulent viscera
of life. Even now I plot what I will take as mine.

Zelda Fitzgerald

A Dozen or So Reasons for Marrying Scott Fitzgerald Interspersed with Lines by Edna St. Vincent Millay

Because he was blowy clean—as if each morning
he was washed by the wind.

Because he smelled like new goods.

Because he looked like a jonquil and because we both
had gold-leaf hair and chameleon eyes: blue,
green, sometimes confederate gray.

    yellow forsythia / Holds its breath and will not bloom

Because he believed he would be one of the greatest
writers that ever lived.

Because he smuggled me a bottle of gin into the bone dry
ballroom that was Alabama.

Because he would have laughed when I slipped
out of my flesh-colored swimsuit and did a swan dive
from the high board.

    I throw bright time to chickens in an untidy yard

"Oh, say can you see," he was named after that patriot
who wrote *The Star Spangled Banner.*

Not because he wanted me to be his princess in a tower.
Princess, yes. Tower? Forget the tower.

Because Mrs. Francesca's Ouija board said we were soul
mates and should be married.

We'll live in New York he told me and sent me a map
of Manhattan with a red dot where we'd live. We'll travel
to Paris he promised.

And life goes on forever like the gnawing of a mouse

Because I was his "top girl" and he made me
a heroine in his story.

Because he sent me a flamingo-colored feather fan,
a diamond and platinum wristwatch, a white orchid
corsage and a pink-and-helpless sweater.

Because he moved with the grace of a fencer
dueling with his shadow.

Grief of grief has drained me clean

Because our colors blend and we'll look good "hanging beside each other in the gallery of life."

Zelda Fitzgerald Contributes to Favorite Recipes of Famous Women, 1922

Breakfast:

See if there is any

bacon, and if there is

ask the cook

which pan to fry it in.

Then ask if there are eggs,

and if so

try

and persuade the cook

to poach two of them.

It is better

not to attempt toast,

as it burns

very easily.

Also, in the case of bacon

do not turn the fire too high,

or you

will have to leave

the house

for a week.

Serve

preferably on china plates,

although gold

or wood

will do if handy.

Zelda Fitzgerald Is Banned from Baby Scottie's Baptism, St. Paul, Minnesota, 1921

This damn place is 18 below.
If I were to venture outside, my breast milk
would freeze. Nanny Shirley, repelled by breasts,
prefers formula dispensed in bottles.

Mama nursed me till I was old enough
to chaw on a chicken bone. If I tell Nanny Shirley,
will she faint with the bone of disgust
lodged in her throat?

Scott insists the baby be baptized Catholic
in the ice palace of the Visitation Convent chapel.
I am confined to our home igloo for fear
of outrageous behavior. Might I expose

a milk-gorged breast to Father Eskimo
or to one of the Fitzgerald puritans?
But Baby Scottie approves of me. Skin
scented of pear blossom, her lips

soft as magnolia buds. The pink shield
of her hand raised to my chest,
her foot taps against my ribs
to the ragtime duet of our hearts.

Zelda Fitzgerald in Hollywood, 1927

Palm trees, poinsettia, parrots,

      pretty houses,

      pretty money

      pretty jewels.

I did not think there were so many

      pretty girls

in the world.

Each day with the sunrise,

      pretty girls

arise, dewy fresh as Venus,

(from some golden shell

created by Samuel Goldwyn

on the back lot of his studio).

They recite their scripted lines

      I am a pretty girl

then dive into a platinum pool

studded with diamonds.

Goofo (the man I call Husband,

Darling Heart, Dearest Love, Deo)

is infatuated with a seventeen-year-old

      pretty girl.

Tonight they are at dinner

(chaperoned by her mother).

Tonight in the bathtub

of our bungalow—ashes, ashes,

all is falling down—I burn

the clothes I designed:

      pretty dresses

      pretty fire

      pretty flames

      pretty boy Scott.

Zelda Fitzgerald's Blue Vase, 1928

Like a fireworks shower crackling
against the sky on July Fourth,

a sound like ice shattering
in one of your gin rickeys,

the Murano vase, a favorite of mine,
thrown against the fireplace.

Even drunk and sobbing
your aim, Scott, was unerring.

Your father is nothing but an Irish cop,
but at least he can hold his liquor.

Wap! Your open hand
slapped my face.

Will this scene, Scott, appear
in one of your stories?

I wiped dripping blood from my nose
and later nursed a black eye.

Zelda Fitzgerald Writes *Save Me the Waltz* in Phipps Clinic, 1932

In this house of the crazy I dance
out of step lost in the choreography of myself:

three, one, two, one, three, two. The doctor frowns
at the faulty wiring of my smile that flashes

without reason. At night a girl screams,
"Murder in the first degree!" During the day

a woman wanders the hall, ghost
in a second-rate detective story.

Once I was a nasturtium. In this hothouse I smell
like the rubbery things that breed here.

From a leaky lifeboat of words I write
for the allowed two hours a day.

But Scott? Scott is a Mad Man on the loose.

My novel, He says, poaches on what is His.
"Our" life is His alone to put on a page

and barter for dollars. I must change my hero's

name, may not imitate His rhythms, am not

to damage His public image. I cannot say
(except to myself):

My book is none of my husband's
Goddamned business.

Sheilah Graham Appraises Her Photograph with Scott Fitzgerald

I, too, have seen the quavering fate destroy
Your destiny's bright spinning
      —Edna St. Vincent Millay

Posed astride the donkey of Destiny

in this Tijuana tourist photograph

I auditioned for the role of Sane and Proper

Wife of F. Scott Fitzgerald.

      (part never officially open)

I'd been content being pleasant scenery.

Then Scott scripted me as *Beloved Infidel.*

Or, was I Eliza Doolittle enrolled

in the College of Fitzgerald?

      (and how did I cast him?)

My smile, look for yourself, is bright

as a Hollywood marquee. Did I believe

I could ride into the City of Marriage

with *caballero* Fitzgerald at my side?

Could I seduce Scott to wear sobriety

with the nonchalance of the sombrero and serape

he wears in this photo? What of Wife Zelda?
Who would write her out of the plot?

      (poor crazy Zelda)

Look again. In the shadows, off to the left,
our backs are turned to a nobody man—
pocketed hands, black suit and bowler.
Only now do I recognize Fate waiting its turn.

Zelda Fitzgerald after a Highland Hospital Excursion to the Circus, Fall 1937

Ladies and Gentlemen,   Doctors in White Coats, Skeptics

and Scoffers, direct your eyes high above the circus ring,

up, up to the top of the tent where I, Miss Zelda,

> *graduate of half-a-dozen mental Institutes*,
> attempt the dangerous feat of walking
> the tightrope of sanity.

I look straight ahead as if traveling again

on the Aquitania bobbing in rough seas

headed for France. The horizon is unreliable.

> Squeamish? Cover your eyes
> and peer through spread fingers.
> I could tumble at any moment.

My safety net is worn and frayed.

Like a cake with too many raisins

I can fall with the weight of myself.

> I've brandished the balance pole of faith
> so often even God yawns open-mouthed.
> Won't you pray for me? No? Well then,

hold your breath as I step out,

foot pointed like a ballerina,

onto the narrow wire of reality.

Georgia O'Keeffe

Georgia O'Keeffe Paints Cebolla Church, 1945

A stovepipe is its steeple. Its cross
a small gesture against the surplus
of sky, the corroding tin roof
of life. In this place window & door
are rationed like gas & tires. Wind

& sand scour & bleach the shadows
hanging from eaves, resting in the recess
of nave & door. Painting is a way to see
the shape of what endures. To the south,
men explode the shape of the future.

I do not like the idea of happiness.
The people of this church know
the white door of happiness
blows shut. We must carry flint
& tinder into dark interior spaces.

Georgia O'Keeffe Hitches a Ride to Abiquiu

after a 1944 photo by Maria Chabot

As if I were Charles Lindbergh setting off for Paris, Maurice gives me his leather helmet. I tuck in my hair, push goggles, his too, to the top of my head and roll up my jeans. I throw one leg over the Harley-Davidson Knucklehead. Maurice says it is important to call the motorcycle by its full and correct name because a machine, this one at least, has a soul and can exact revenge if slighted. My hands bracket Maurice's slim hips. He tromps on the start pedal. We're off.

> fast as dust devils
>
> against the landscape of his back
>
> my smile a mesa

Miss O'Keeffe at the White Place

On the sheer walls of the White Place cliffs,
swallows anchor nests shaped like beehive ovens
at Acoma Pueblo. The birds sprint from spire to spire,
acrobats without net or wire. Today's sky, work-shirt
blue, is backdrop for ash-white palisades.
Can I be as daring as a swallow, trust my eyes
to feel the contours of what holds us aloft,
what binds us to earth?

> open-mouthed gargoyles
> spit desiccated stars
> my hair goes gray

Miss O'Keeffe at the Black Place

This morning the wind is hoarse from rasping

against lava. Last night we roasted venison

over cedar coals. As we lay on our cots

Maria read aloud from *Taras Bulba*, the light

from her lantern a one-eyed coyote crouched

in our small canvas cave. Even a Cossack astride

a sturdy stallion might tremble riding into this wild

country. I call this the Black Place, but it is also gray

and molten pewter layered with white like salt left

when oceans covered this land. I come here to paint

the elephant herd of hills. It is a place that picks clean

the gristle and fat of regret.

> buzzards overhead
>
> in the belly of my shadow
>
> the cat sleeps

Miss O'Keeffe Makes Pea Soup

There is a bit of a bitch
in every good cook
I wrote in the flyleaf
of one of my cookbooks.

My body, that reservoir
of desire, lusts after the freshest peas.
At the thumb's suggestion,
their crisp robes
slide open.

> When my kimono slipped off,
> Stieglitz photographed
> my body,
> supple
> & smooth.

Defend the peas' green identity.
Do not elaborate beyond broth,
onion, mint & salt. This soup
is folk song, not operatic chorus.

> Old men of art wanted
> my paintings muddy

& dismal. Like theirs. I say *flattery*
and criticism go down the same drain
and I am quite free.

Heat the soup slowly—
as slowly as rain clouds collect
along the spine of the Pedernal.
Shower with chives whose bite
ˑreminds me how winter always returns.

    If I were to come back
    in another life,
    I would be a blonde soprano
    singing high, clear notes
    that shatter the bell jar of fear.

In this life I dress in black—
its voice does not argue—
so I can hear the colors of the hills,
& cliffs, the holes of bones,
the blue cadenza of the Chama.

Georgia O'Keeffe Divides the Iris

My hands are knobbed
and brown as these rhizomes;
would they take root
    if buried in the dirt?

Once my hands were calla lilies—
posed and photographed
by Stieglitz, sculpting me with light
    as if I were a mannequin.

I transplanted myself where light
exists without bargaining
in this land of the faraway
    from which there is no return.

As if painting a canvas
I planted this garden with iris.
Estiben dug brown and yellow
    ones from along the acequia.

Now when the iris bloom
I see only edges.
At center, everything
    is ink-stained

the throat of each iris

a black door

the periphery of petals

      life's fragrant deception.

Lauren Bacall Shares a Limousine to the Afterlife with Robin Williams

after Amorak Huey

The limousine is the oyster gray

of early-morning mist. It glides

to the curb in the only parking space

for blocks. The back door opens.

I slide in next to Robin. He is dressed

in faded sweats like he's just come from a workout

at the gym. His eyes are closed. Maybe

he was dozing, waiting for me

to be done with the last details of death.

Robin and I have never met, but no matter,

we've ended up in this vehicle

by virtue of our departure times.

Robin turns to me, hands me a beat-up tin soldier.

"Don't you love the patina of old toy

soldiers?" he says. I wish I'd brought

a carnation from the graveyard

to give to him. Then I could tell him

about the soap my mother bathed

me with as a child. I could tell him how the man

with palsied hands at the corner convenience store

orders the same soap for me. The driver's shadow

is just visible through the glass that divides the cab

from the passenger compartment. The radio

is tuned to a gospel station where Louis Armstrong

plays *When the Saints Come Marching In.*

In seconds we are out of the city

cruising along small-town streets

where a few people wave from the sidewalk.

I like that Robin doesn't feel compelled

to make me smile. I don't bother to put on lipstick.

We lean a bit. Our shoulders touch.

Mr. Wizard,

Consider this a warning, you weasel.
Next week I appear on "The View" &
in case it skipped your mind, I am 15.
Once Whoopi G. gets wind of your
sleight-of-hand behind that curtain
you'll be hiring a squad of winged
monkeys. And surfing the web for
wizard-size ruby red slippers. Click
'til your heels blister, buster. You're
about to be sucked up by a tornado.

Dorothy

After Dorothy Gale's Mid-Life Crisis

Lulled and dulled by the fragrance
from red poppy fields, my mid-life crisis
retreat to Oz morphed into full time

resident status & eventually a place
in the Yellow Brick Road Home
for Seniors. We aging ones were drying up

like tumbleweeds about to skitter
across the plains & pile up along
the orange plastic fence at the edge

of the freeway. But the Wizard's men
from the Bureau of Eternal Life filmed
& photoshopped us with their rose-

colored lens for Oz Retirement Lifestyle ads.
Our morning paper arrived scissored
& redacted. Sometimes a line would remain:

"Memorials may be made to—"
The Muzak in the halls kept us on hold.
Late at night I'd occasionally hear

distant strains of staff radios—Patsy Cline

asking "Who's sorry now?" Hell,

me for one.

Per conditions of my release I can't

tell you any details about my transfer

back to Kansas. I can tell you what a relief

it is to hear wind exhale around the corners

of the home like a minor key harmonica.

What a comfort to see grain elevators

like grey cathedrals against the sky. I admit

I look away when the lab technician slides

the needle into my vein for a blood sample.

But when the final cyclone heads my way,

here I can see it coming & hold out both arms.

Faye Wray Tweets atop the Empire State Building

Call off planes. Cops 2. Screams misunderstood.

In good hands. KK & I signed contract 4 new reality show.

#LoveStoriesFromHighestHeights

Elizabeth Barrett Takes Up Tweeting

@Lizbarrett

Robert, dear one, I have found a new way for us
to send messages. It's called tweeting, perhaps because
it's short and sweet? Papa will nev

@Lizbarrett

er catch on. Papa wants a sum toted in pen
and ink. Messages sent by unseen forces
wld not tally in his ledger. Tweeting takes a bit of p

@Lizbarrett

ractice as one is limited to 140 characters
per message. 140 & not a letter or space more.
Didn't @WillShakespeare call brevity the soul

@Lizbarrett

of wit? So luv let us outwit Papa who wld prefer
I spend the remainder of my life as a lapdog
like my own dear Flush—docile & cosseted &

@Lizbarrett

obedient 2 commands: Heel. Stay! Sit. Speak.
Quiet. Oh, enough barking. Robert, I want to escape
Papa's leash & walk in the park on paths

@Lizbarrett

far from London, beyond England

where the sun is as warm and luxuriant

as our love. "Am I never to see Italy with my eyes?"

Say Yes.

@Lizbarrett

Say, Yes, we shall see it together. Do not

remind me, gentle one, that you advocated

such escape many times & ways. #Letmecounttheways.

@Lizbarrett

I am finding all this counting a bit taxing.

Let me just say I accept your proposal of marriage

& propose we escape to Italy as soon as

Emily Dickinson Introduces Her Blog

Propelled by chance's cosmic pull
This Thing called Internet
Allows me from my garret space
To publish this gazette.

Perhaps I'll speak of solitude:
Its subtle change of hue
From morning's white immensity
To evening's black adieu.

I might discuss Nothing with you—
And how to wear its coat,
Or how to spurn ego's offer
Of Fame's promissory note.

I could divulge my recipe
For fudge or gingerbread.
A poet demands sustenance
To say what must be said.

To Death—embezzler of joy—I'll
Deny a starring role.
Assign it to the anteroom
In deference to the Soul.

My Letters to the World appear

On registered domain—

Inspect my cryptic dashes, please—

As signals from my brain.

Emily Dickinson Observes Lent

Employed with brash humility
The Dash has served me well.
Beneath its mask of brevity
Vast paradoxes dwell.

Enamored with the blazing dash
And its electric voice
Devotion asks I offer it
As Lenten sacrifice.

Then Comma curled upon my lap
Content to purr, to sleep
Wherever it was bid, meek chap,
Too Fraidy Cat to Leap.

Surprise! The Exclamation Point!
That breathless knight with sword
Unsheathed! Consumed by thrust and shout!
How tiresome! On guard!

The Question Mark asks why? And why?
When queries come pell-mell
Resounding in that single ear
Whose brain will first rebel?

The Colon stands upright and primed:
To set apart a quote,
To cleave named chapter from said verse,
To launch a list: take note.

The Period with one swift blow
Can nail wild wonder shut.
Arrest the breath. And mimic death.
That haughty tyrant dot.

The Dash—now resurrected—now
White deprivation—done
Will there be cube and sphere enough
To comprehend—the sum?

Venus de Milo Gets Ready for the Halloween Party

The missing arms were a dead giveaway.
I'd need sleeves to cover youthful sins.
No way did I want to party talk with therapist types
about how I'd given my left arm
for love of some bozo whose helmet
glinted in the sun, shield held provocatively
to protect natural endowments.

Explaining the loss of the right was even more likely
to provoke, *How do you feel about that?*
Only the most beautiful of women believed
my answer: *I'd had it with the adoration bit.*
Drastic action was called for.

Witch, I thought as soon as I opened the invite.
Medusa, I decided after sleeping on the idea.
Medusa, too, had done a beauty-pedestal gig
until Athena got miffed, turned her tresses
to snakes and trashed her good looks—
making her sooo ugly anyone who looked into her
eyes turned to stone.

One night off from paragon-of-beauty duty,
I told myself as I dressed: black lipstick,

shades, atop my head a hundred writhing snakes
with glow-in-the-dark fangs, black gown with sleeves
flapping like wings of a vampire bat.

But habit hewn in marble is oh, so hard, to break.
I walked out the door, party bound,
one beautiful breast exposed.

The Little Mermaid at the Aquatic Arts Academy (AAA)

Accordion music or maybe an arrow-to-the-heart
ballad would be an apt soundtrack to my potholed

career path. Take, for example, that stint at a reception
desk. I called it entry-level traffic guard, although Ms.

Employment Counselor described the role as voice-and-
face-of-the-corporation. Turned out my whole

gestalt was a mismatch. I smiled like a Cheshire cat
hovering over an open tin of caviar as documented on

instant replay video. So, no surprise, I was summarily
jettisoned from that corporate ship. Digging in my castoff

knapsack of talents I unpacked that latent dream:
Lounge Singer. You know, sitting sexy on a piano like

Madonna as Breathless Mahoney in silver lamé coaxing no-
nonsense Dick Tracy, the hunky Mr. Beatty, to let his body

oooh, go with the flow, baby. My sultry voice, however
promising in the shower, sank in the noisy jungle

quicksand of lounge chatter and clinking ice cubes.

Rescue came at last when an undercover mermaid

support group intervened and splish, splash

threw me into the saltwater pool at the Triple A.

Underwater, a vortex whirled away my vocational

vampires. The Academy hired me to teach Senior Swim,

Water Baby Level Two and Marathon Swim Skills for

X-treme Athletes. We swam, old and jelly-limbed

young, novice and expert, immersed in that fluid

zone where body becomes buoyant vessel.

Advisory Letter: Little Mermaid to
Errant Lover

Astrologically, our destiny was to float the ocean of bliss.

Both of us water signs, skilled at navigating life's erratic

currents. Me, Cancer, flirty and friendly as a SeaWorld

dolphin performing for a hunk of raw flesh. You, Scorpio,

elusive and electric as the eels in the saltwater tank at

Four Treasures in Chinatown where Mr. Yee mixes

Gimlets for Lovers (adding one tiny drop of bitters) their

house specialty. In my experience, love needs secret

ingredients. I'm a fingers-crossed gal who wears a lucky

jackalope foot on a lanyard so I can stroke its soft

karmic powers in times of need. Like now, reviewing

laundry lists of your deep-water indiscretions.

Mermaids (you didn't know?) live for 300 years, so run the

numbers. Singlehandedly I could go through a veritable

ocean of men which is likely to earn me poison

pen letters and a cache of flame mail despite

quantum meruit. Fellini said it was easier to be faithful to
restaurants than a woman. I'd edit the gender to man.

Scorpio man, eel man, here's da plan. I'll book our old
table at Four Treasures where my guy, Mr. Yee, will

undertake plying you with gimlets, the double bitters
version. Their side effects—print too fine to read—include

weeping a Pacific Ocean of remorse. Till then,
expect all future horoscopes and fortune cookies to read:

*Yada, yada, yada. Cinch up your Speedo. If you wanna play
Zeus, you gotta synchronize your strokes.* Call me.

Rapunzel Brings Her Women's Studies Class to the Tower

The setup looked so innocent. Like a rustic

storybook estate. Before you ask, the ivy escape route

now clambering up the walls was tended

by an apprentice of Edward Scissorhands.

The Government was reclaiming this tract

for a planned wilderness. It was so quiet

      I could hear my hair grow. Occasionally

a crazed scientist would wander by, eyes

to the ground, mapping endangered four-leaf clover.

I was endangered too, but had signed on to relinquish

the rib of victimhood. I thought life could be arranged

so only my favorite pineapple LifeSavers came up

in the assorted roll. One sleeve at a time, I slipped

out of my coat sewn from sackcloth and shadows

      to wear the skin of solitude.

Each day I recited that line from Rilke:

Let this darkness be a bell tower and you the bell.

When I came down from the tower, the media wanted

a country western song. Everyone would hum,

wipe away a tear, then sing aloud the verse

where Wrong crashes its vintage pickup. Instead,

I uncoiled my crown of braids, cut the ties and loosened

the strands that held my story captive. Every day

      new towers of darkness rise. Do I need to say

your voices are searchlights that can sweep the horizon

to reveal fault lines and illuminate passage?

Janis Joplin

Janis Joplin Buys Her First Record Albums

The wind is tied to a stake in this town. My foot
is caught in the same loop and I am thirsty

for the solace of rebellion. How much of life
can you see when the highest place in town

is a water tower? Getting high in this town
means walking to the top of the Rainbow Bridge—

high enough to let a Navy destroyer pass under.
When I climb onto the catwalk and let my legs

dangle and swing over the side, blue lights flash,
the police arrive. For God's sake, this is not

how I will leave town. At sea level my breath escapes
like car exhaust. The air smells of sulfur

and my skin is singed. I would go up in flames
without the albums of Leadbelly and Bessie Smith.

I hop the freight-train of their voices, ride someplace
where being me is a song not yet written.

Dear Janis,

Happy Birthday, gypsy-footed daughter,
my daughter of turtle blues, flying needle,
my wildcat oil well daughter.

I've sent a box of birthday candles
and one extra to make twenty-five.
I've sent a pan of your favorite brownies.
Uncut so they stay a bit gooey.

Yesterday you were seven, riding
that blue bike too fast around
the cul-de-sac, coming to me
to paint your knees with mercurochrome.

I dreamt the ladies at bridge club
passed around photos of grandchildren.
I handed each a 45 record of you singing
"Down on Me." None of them

had a *Port Arthur News* reporter
photograph their family at Christmas
like we did. Rock and roll trumps
babies for some. Calendar pages flip

too fast. I'll lie on the sofa a bit,

then start dinner for your Dad, Laura

and Mike. Wish you were here.

We're having meatloaf with pepper jelly.

Love, Mother

Self-Portrait as Janis Joplin's Porsche

Sometimes it's not enough
to be your oyster gray self. Not enough
to travel through life, a metaphor
for sex and speed.

If you can't be loved for yourself,
do you settle for being loved for who
you're with?

That funky paint job was Janis'
psychedelic scream to the universe:
Hey, see me! Hear me! Her fans
slid their hands over every inch of my body
as if I could grant wishes. They scribbled
notes of devotion on scraps of paper
and anchored them under the wiper blades.

The only thing to do? Floor it.
The other thing to do? Listen
to the radio while Janis ripped
out pieces of her heart, threw them
like candy along a parade route.

Janis Joplin's Lynx Coat

I stole this fur from an animal wilder
than me. To sharpen my tongue and claws,
I guzzle Southern Comfort full tilt. Rose-tinted
shades can't disguise my descent into the blues.

Let's not pretend I'm beautiful in this coat.
When I was a kid, mother dressed me
like a model in the Simplicity pattern catalog:
ruffles, puffy sleeves, skirts with petticoats.

I was not beautiful even then.
Beautiful is just another word that starts with "b."
I'd rather be famous, just another word
that starts with "f." Wearing a coat like this

means no one dares ask questions
I don't want to answer. I take this coat to bed,
a lover still beside me come morning.
Why am I so damn cold? Cold, ever colder.

The Last Time I Saw Janis Joplin

She looked as if she was still waiting

for somebody to give her a Mercedes Benz.

She clutched a damp take-a-ticket stub

two chairs ahead in the lineup

outside the Social Security Office.

You thought she was dead? Me, too.

But there she was, filing for bennies.

That roadhouse voice was my tip off.

How was she looking? *Oh, baby, baby,*

baby, baby—her skin had long lost

its southern comfort. Sequins puddled

at her feet from a tatty gold vest.

Her hair was on a binge, so frizzed

out on freedom the guy next to her

kept twitching, and finally got up

and left. I slid into his chair just as the clock

turned five of five. They called her number.

As they shooed me out, she grabbed my hand

and whispered, *I was buried alive in the blues.*

Marilyn Monroe

What Marilyn Monroe Tells Her Dressmaker While Fitting Her "Mr. President" Gown

I want it to fit me like the skin

of a peach, the scales of a fish,

the glove of a surgeon, like whiskey

in a silver flask, the pop of flashbulbs.

Yes, like smoke on a magician's mirror,

like fog hugging San Francisco Bay.

It should fit smooth as the glide

of a snake. Does a snake wear

underwear? Neither do I.

I want this dress slinky as a Freudian slip.

I want every curve in the road

of my body to signal danger.

I don't care if I have to pant

to sing "Happy Birthday, Mr. President."

I want Joe DiMaggio to pant. I want

Arthur Miller's tongue to hang out.

Ditto Bobby Kennedy. Pull

those stitches a bit tighter. I want

every man in Madison Square Garden

breathless.

Marilyn Monroe Imagines Her Life as Menu Items at Schrafft's

Tomato Aspic

I was an abandoned passenger, my father
a train departed before I was born. My mother's
mind softened like aspic unmolded on a warm plate.
She took to wearing a nurse's white uniform
believing she had power to cure illness.
In Rockhaven Sanitarium mother said, "Radio waves
are destroying my brain."

      From the orphanage window
the RKO Studio sign—tower atop globe—
beamed bright waves on me.

Chopped Egg Sandwich

American sex goddess, innocent
as white bread with trimmed crusts.
That was who I agreed to be. My eyes
      stayed Norma Jeane blue,
but the rest of me? My hair was a scraggly field.
It was straightened, bleached, dyed,
shaped, trimmed, permed. Makeup
camouflaged the bump on my nose.
My dumpling chin was sculpted

and I was renamed.

Clam Chowder

My gum line was too high. To conceal
      its indecent pink
I was coached to lower
my upper lip when smiling. I practiced
before the mirror, my lip quivering
like a child eating chowder with a fork.

White Angel

Truman Capote and I drank
White Angels—half gin, half vodka.
Truman kept his hands
around the drink.
      I was his *beautiful child.*
When we danced he held
my wrist so I wouldn't get lost.
If I were Snow White, then he was Gossip,
my witty dwarf.

Apple Pie

In my favorite poem of his, Mr. Yeats cautioned,
never give all the heart. I laid down a crust

over what was bruised and blighted.

Drawn by the scent of sweet cinnamon,

men ordered me: dessert à la mode.

    None of them the father.

Moth from the moon pinned to the past—

attempting escape, I tore myself apart.

Marilyn Monroe Sits for Andy Warhol
in the Afterlife

Andy stands behind the easel, toothpaste-white

tennis shoes visible. He wants to paint me

as an act of forgiveness

for selling my lips like carnival booth prizes

and shelving my image

like a can of tomato soup.

But the paper bags of his lungs

collapse with sobs. I lead him to the blue chair

of happiness where I sat. He imagines

he can re-film the scene where he hid under the bed

and refused to go to his father's wake. Instead, I comb

his baby-bird hair with my fingers the way a mother does.

Opening his shirt, he asks me to bless

the bullet wound and scars on his chest

that resemble, he says,

a Byzantine cross.

Instead, I take the brush from the easel

and touch

its sable hairs to his forehead, nose, eyelids, ears.

We are here, I tell him, *to learn to be ourselves.*

It's not as easy as it sounds.

Above the blue chair

a thumbtacked notice

with curled corners:

Chair Can Collapse Without Warning.

I dip the brush in crimson paint, stroke color

like antiseptic on Andy's chest. With Venetian gold

Andy paints the suspension bridge

of my clavicle, up the throat's ladder

onto the cliff of my chin.

For now, we are the calm

and chaos of sunrise and sunset,

the shimmer of amber,

the roar from the lion's mouth.

Notes

Casa Azul: Casa Azul is the house where Frida Kahlo was born and died.

Frida Kahlo Prepares an Altar for Día de los Inocentes: *Dia de los Inocentes,* Day of the Innocents, is part of the Day of the Dead festivities in Mexico.

Frida and Frankenstein: Frida Kahlo became a fan of American movies when she was in New York City with Diego Rivera in 1933.

The Ballad Of Frida And Diego: The paintings referenced in the ballad are:

> *Diego and Frida 1929-1944,* 1944, an anniversary gift for Diego.
> *A Few Small Nips,* 1935, painted after Diego's affair with Cristina.
> *The Two Fridas,* 1939, completed at the time of Frida and Diego's divorce.
> *Long Live Life,* 1954, Frida's last painting, completed shortly before her death.

Confession of Sarah Rosetta Wakeman, Also Known as Private Lyons Wakeman, 153rd Regiment, New York State Volunteers, Union Army: Italicized language is taken from *An Uncommon Soldier: The Civil War*

Letters of Sarah Rosetta Wakeman, alias Pvt. Lyons Wakeman, 153rd Regiment, New York State Volunteers, 1862-1864. Edited by Lauren Cook Burgess.

Nurses of Bataan, Prisoners of War, The Third Year. Based on *We Band of Angels: The Untold Story of American Nurses Trapped on Bataan by the Japanese*, Elizabeth M. Norman, Random House, 1999.

Lucy Audubon in the Boarding House, 1865: "I have under errour and ignorance sacrificed" is a quote from Lucy Audubon's letter to a relative.

Before Her Round-the-World Flight Amelia Visits With a Psychic: It was Amelia Earhart's practice to write what she called "pop off" letters before any major flight.

Maman: Spider facts are taken from *Spiders: The Ultimate Predators* by Stephen Dalton and *The World of Spiders* by Adrienne Mason.

Zelda Fitzgerald Contributes to Favorite Recipes of Famous Women, 1922: This is a found poem from *Favorite Recipes of Famous Women*, ed. Florence Stratton, Harper, 1925.

Zelda Fitzgerald Is Banned from Baby Scottie's Baptism, St. Paul, Minnesota, 1921: Quoted language is from the Zelda Fitzgerald biography by Sally Cline.

Zelda Fitzgerald after a Highland Hospital Excursion to the Circus, Fall 1937: Quoted lines are from letters by Zelda to Scott Fitzgerald.

Georgia O'Keeffe Paints Cebolla Church, 1945: The first atomic bomb was detonated in July 1945, in the Southern New Mexico desert. The quote is from a letter by Georgia O'Keeffe to Anita Pollitzer.

Miss O'Keeffe Makes Pea Soup: The quote by Georgia O'Keeffe appears in "A Studio Book" published by The Viking Press 1976.

Georgia O'Keeffe Divides the Iris: The quote is from a 1929 letter from Georgia O'Keefe to Alfred Stieglitz.

Marilyn Monroe Imagines Her Life as Menu Items at Schrafft's: Truman Capote wrote a memoir of Marilyn entitled *The Beautiful Child*.

About the Author

Susan J. Erickson happened on poetry. After vowing to stop talking about writing a long-intended mystery novel, she enrolled in a poetry correspondence course offered by Western Washington University, reasoning that even an alternate genre would stimulate writing. It did. That course led to others and eventually to this book, *Lauren Bacall Shares a Limousine*, the winner of the Brick Road Poetry Prize. Poetry is now her genre of choice.

Susan grew up in the Midwest in a Garrison Keillor setting. She attended the University of Minnesota, earning a B.S. and M.S. She now lives in Bellingham, Washington, and marvels at living on the edge of the sea under the looming presence of an active volcano.

Erickson speaks to the decisions women make in life, how they live with those decisions and the justifications offered for their behavior. She also explores how physical beauty can impact a person's life. Even though poems in this volume are in the voice of other women, Susan acknowledges that they sometimes reflect her own life experiences as well. The poems in *Lauren Bacall Shares a Limousine* give voice to women both well and little known, illuminating moments in their lives that dramatize the inheritance of silence many women still face. Poems from the series appear in *2River View, Crab Creek Review, Museum of Americana, The Fourth River, The James Franco Review, The Tishman Review* and in anthologies such as *Till The Tide: An Anthology of Mermaid Poetry*.

Erickson is also a collage artist and has created a unique series of cards using postage stamp images of the women represented in her poems.

Egress Studio Press published her chapbook, *The Art of Departure*. Susan helped establish the Sue C. Boynton Poetry Walk and

Contest in Whatcom County and has served on its committee since its inception in 2006. Visit her at www.susanjerickson.com.

Our Mission

The mission of Brick Road Poetry Press is to publish and promote poetry that entertains, amuses, edifies, and surprises a wide audience of appreciative readers. We are not qualified to judge who deserves to be published, so we concentrate on publishing what we enjoy. Our preference is for poetry geared toward dramatizing the human experience in language rich with sensory image and metaphor, recognizing that poetry can be, at one and the same time, both familiar as the perspiration of daily labor and as outrageous as a carnival sideshow.

BRICK ROAD
POETRY PRESS

Also Available from Brick Road Poetry Press
www.brickroadpoetrypress.com

Etch and Blur by Jamie Thomas

Water-Rites by Ann E. Michael

Bad Behavior by Michael Steffen

Tracing the Lines by Susanna Lang

Rising to the Rim by Carol Tyx

Treading Water with God by Veronica Badowski

Rich Man's Son by Ron Self

Just Drive by Robert Cooperman

The Alp at the End of My Street by Gary Leising

The Word in Edgewise by Sean M. Conrey

Household Inventory by Connie Jordan Green

Practice by Richard M. Berlin

A Meal Like That by Albert Garcia

Cracker Sonnets by Amy Wright

Things Seen by Joseph Stanton

Battle Sleep by Shannon Tate Jonas

BRICK ROAD

POETRY PRESS

Also Available from Brick Road Poetry Press
www.brickroadpoetrypress.com

Dancing on the Rim by Clela Reed

Possible Crocodiles by Barry Marks

Pain Diary by Joseph D. Reich

Otherness by M. Ayodele Heath

Drunken Robins by David Oates

Damnatio Memoriae by Michael Meyerhofer

Lotus Buffet by Rupert Fike

The Melancholy MBA by Richard Donnelly

Two-Star General by Grey Held

Chosen by Toni Thomas

About the Prize

The Brick Road Poetry Prize, established in 2010, is awarded annually for the best book-length poetry manuscript. Entries are accepted August 1st through November 1st. The winner receives $1000 and publication. For details on our preferences and the complete submission guidelines, please visit our website at www.brickroadpoetrypress.com.